I0696145

"IoT for Starters: Exploring the Connected World" is a comprehensive guide that introduces beginners to the vast and evolving realm of the Internet of Things (IoT). This book offers a detailed yet accessible overview of IoT technology, its applications, and its impact on various industries.

The book starts by elucidating the fundamental concepts of IoT, explaining how everyday objects are interconnected through sensors, software, and network connectivity to collect and exchange data. It delves into the underlying technologies powering IoT, including sensors, actuators, communication protocols, and cloud computing.

Readers are guided through real-world examples and case studies that demonstrate the practical applications of IoT across diverse sectors such as healthcare, agriculture, manufacturing, smart homes, and transportation. These examples showcase how IoT enhances efficiency, productivity, and convenience while also addressing challenges and considerations like security, privacy, and interoperability.

The book emphasizes the importance of data analytics and visualization in deriving actionable insights from the massive amounts of data generated by IoT devices. Additionally, the book highlights the significance of standards and best practices in developing reliable and scalable IoT solutions.

Furthermore, "IoT for Starters" provides guidance for entrepreneurs and startups looking to venture into the IoT space. It offers advice on developing a viable IoT business model and leveraging emerging trends in the field.

Overall, this book serves as a primer for individuals with limited prior knowledge of IoT, offering them a foundational understanding of its concepts, applications, and potential, making it an invaluable resource for beginners looking to explore the connected world of IoT.

Table of Contents

Chapter 1: Introduction to the Internet of Things (IoT)

The Internet of Things, commonly abbreviated as IoT, is a technological revolution that has been transforming the way we interact with the world around us. It's a concept that promises to make our lives more convenient, efficient, and interconnected than ever before. In this essay, we'll explore the fundamentals of IoT, its origins, key components, and its potential impact on various aspects of our daily lives.

Origins of IoT

The concept of connecting physical objects to the internet can be traced back to the early 1980s, when the idea of a "smart" Coke machine at Carnegie Mellon University, capable of reporting its inventory and temperature, was conceived. However, it wasn't until the late 1990s and early 2000s that the term "Internet of Things" began to gain traction. Kevin Ashton, a British technology pioneer, coined the term in 1999 while working on radio-frequency identification (RFID) technology. His vision was to use RFID tags to track and manage physical objects seamlessly. It gained significant attention in the early 2000s as the cost of sensors and connectivity devices began to decrease significantly. The idea was to enable everyday objects and devices to communicate and share data over the internet, creating a network of interconnected things.

What is IoT?

At its core, IoT refers to the connection of physical objects or "things" to the internet, allowing them to collect and exchange data. These "things" can range from household appliances and wearable devices to industrial machines and vehicles. Through sensors, actuators, and embedded technology, these objects can gather information from their surroundings and communicate that data to other devices or central systems.

The Evolution of IoT: From Concept to Connectivity

The Internet of Things (IoT) has undergone a remarkable evolution over the past few decades, transforming from a visionary concept into a pervasive and transformative technology that impacts nearly every facet of modern life. This essay explores the evolution of IoT, tracing its origins, key milestones, and the profound changes it has brought to our world.

Key Milestones in IoT Evolution:

1. **Advancements in Sensor Technology:** The development of affordable and efficient sensors marked a pivotal moment in IoT evolution. These sensors could collect data such as temperature, humidity, light, and motion, allowing everyday objects to become "smart."

2. **Proliferation of Wireless Connectivity:** The expansion of wireless communication technologies, including Wi-Fi, Bluetooth, and cellular networks, provided the necessary infrastructure for IoT devices to connect and communicate seamlessly.

3. **IPv6 Adoption:** The transition to IPv6, with its vastly expanded address space, was a critical enabler of IoT growth. IPv6 allows for a virtually unlimited number of unique IP addresses, essential for accommodating the massive number of IoT devices.

4. **Cloud Computing:** The emergence of cloud computing platforms provided scalable and cost-effective solutions for storing, processing, and analyzing the vast amounts of data generated by IoT devices.

5. **Standardization Efforts:** Various organizations and consortia, such as the IoT Consortium, have worked on establishing industry standards and protocols for IoT, promoting interoperability and security.

6. **Edge Computing:** Edge computing emerged as a complementary paradigm to cloud computing, enabling data processing and decision-making closer to the source of data, reducing latency and improving real-time capabilities.

7. **Machine Learning and AI Integration:** IoT data analytics became more sophisticated with the integration of machine learning and artificial intelligence, enabling predictive maintenance, anomaly detection, and personalized user experiences.

Why is IoT Important?

The Importance of IoT: Shaping the Connected Future

The Internet of Things (IoT) has emerged as one of the most significant technological revolutions of the 21st century, fundamentally changing the way we interact with our surroundings, businesses operate, and society's function. In this essay, we explore the importance of IoT, examining the multifaceted impacts it has on our lives, industries, and the global economy.

1. Enhanced Efficiency and Productivity: IoT plays a pivotal role in enhancing efficiency and productivity across various sectors. In industries, it enables predictive maintenance of machinery, reducing downtime and preventing costly breakdowns. In agriculture, precision farming based on IoT data optimizes resource usage and crop yield. In smart cities, IoT helps manage traffic flow, reduce energy consumption, and streamline public services.

2. Improved Quality of Life: IoT has a direct impact on our daily lives, making them more convenient and comfortable. Smart homes equipped with IoT devices enable remote control of appliances, energy savings, and enhanced security. Wearable IoT devices monitor health parameters, supporting early detection of medical issues and promoting a healthier lifestyle.

3. Healthcare Advancements: IoT has revolutionized healthcare through remote patient monitoring, telemedicine, and personalized medicine. It allows patients to receive continuous care, reduces the burden on healthcare facilities, and enables doctors to make data-driven decisions for better treatment outcomes.

4. Environmental Sustainability: In the face of climate change and environmental challenges, IoT contributes to sustainability efforts. Environmental sensors monitor air and water quality, predict natural disasters, and aid in wildlife conservation. Smart grid technology optimizes energy distribution, reducing wastage and greenhouse gas emissions.

5. Data-Driven Decision-Making: IoT generates vast amounts of data, which, when analyzed, provides valuable insights. Businesses can make informed decisions based on real-time data, improving customer experiences, optimizing supply chains, and identifying market trends. Governments can use IoT data for urban planning and disaster response.

6. Economic Growth and Job Creation: The IoT ecosystem has become a source of economic growth and job creation. It has spurred innovation in hardware, software, and connectivity technologies, leading to the emergence of startups and new industries. The demand for skilled IoT professionals has also risen, creating job opportunities.

7. Connectivity and Accessibility: IoT connects people and devices globally, breaking down geographical barriers. This connectivity has the potential to bridge the digital divide by providing internet access to remote and underserved areas, thus promoting inclusivity and equitable development.

8. Smart Infrastructure: IoT contributes to the development of smart infrastructure, including smart grids, transportation systems, and buildings. These technologies optimize resource usage, reduce maintenance costs, and enhance the overall resilience and sustainability of infrastructure.

9. Safety and Security: IoT enhances safety and security by enabling real-time monitoring and response. Surveillance systems, fire alarms, and emergency services benefit from IoT technology, ensuring faster and more effective responses to critical situations.

10. Innovation and Future Potential: IoT continues to evolve, and its potential is boundless. As it integrates with artificial intelligence, 5G networks, and quantum computing, it will drive further innovation in areas such as autonomous vehicles, augmented reality, and smart manufacturing.

Key Components of IoT:

1. **Sensors and Actuators:** These are the eyes and hands of IoT. Sensors collect data from the physical world, such as temperature, humidity, light, motion, and more. Actuators, on the other hand, can perform actions based on the data received, like turning on a fan when a room gets too hot.

2. **Connectivity:** IoT devices need a way to transmit data. This is achieved through various connectivity technologies such as Wi-Fi, Bluetooth, cellular networks, and low-power, wide-area networks (LPWAN). The choice of connectivity depends on the specific requirements of the IoT application.

3. **Data Processing and Storage:** The collected data needs to be processed and often stored for analysis. Cloud computing and edge computing play crucial roles in managing and analyzing this data.

4. **User Interface:** IoT applications typically have user interfaces, either in the form of mobile apps or web dashboards, to allow users to monitor and control connected devices remotely.

Chapter 2: IoT Technologies

IoT Sensors and Actuators: The Backbone of the Connected World

The Internet of Things (IoT) has emerged as a transformative force, reshaping industries, cities, and our daily lives. At the heart of this technological revolution are IoT sensors and actuators, the unsung heroes that enable everyday objects to become "smart." In this essay, we will explore the essential roles played by sensors and actuators in IoT, their types, applications, and their profound impact on our connected world.

1. Understanding IoT Sensors:

IoT sensors are the eyes of the IoT ecosystem. They are devices that collect data from the physical world and convert it into a form that can be processed and analyzed by computers or other IoT devices. These sensors come in various types, each designed to detect specific environmental parameters:

- **Temperature Sensors:** Monitor temperature changes in the environment.
- **Humidity Sensors:** Measure moisture levels in the air.
- **Motion Sensors:** Detect movement or changes in position.
- **Light Sensors:** Measure light intensity or ambient light levels.
- **Proximity Sensors:** Detect the presence or absence of objects.
- **Pressure Sensors:** Measure changes in pressure.
- **Gas Sensors:** Detect the presence and concentration of gases.
- **Other Specialized Sensors:** Include sensors for sound, vibration, and more.

These sensors' function based on various principles such as resistance changes, light absorption, piezoelectric effects, or electromagnetic induction. They are often integrated with wireless communication technologies, allowing them to transmit data to central systems or other IoT devices.

2. IoT Actuators:

IoT actuators are the hands of the IoT ecosystem. They are responsible for taking actions based on the data collected by sensors or user commands. Actuators can be thought of as devices that physically interact with the environment to perform specific tasks. Common types of actuators include:

- **Motors:** Used to drive physical movement.

- **Solenoids:** Control valve and switch mechanisms.
- **Valves:** Regulate the flow of fluids or gases.
- **Relays:** Switch electrical circuits on and off.
- **Piezoelectric Actuators:** Produce mechanical motion when voltage is applied.

These actuators are crucial for implementing automated processes and making real-world changes based on the information gathered by sensors. For example, a temperature sensor in a smart thermostat can trigger an actuator (a heating element) to adjust the room temperature.

3. Sensors and Actuators in IoT Systems:

IoT sensors and actuators form the foundation of IoT systems, and they work together seamlessly to bring intelligence and automation to various applications. Here's how they function in an IoT ecosystem:

- **Data Acquisition:** Sensors collect data from the physical world, such as environmental conditions, user inputs, or machine statuses.
- **Data Processing:** The collected data is processed and analyzed, often in real-time, to derive meaningful insights or trigger actions.
- **Decision-Making:** Based on the data analysis, decisions are made either autonomously by the IoT system or through user-defined rules.
- **Actuation:** Actuators execute physical actions or changes in response to the decisions made, affecting the environment or machinery.

4. Applications of Sensors and Actuators in IoT:

The applications of IoT sensors and actuators are wide-ranging and have a profound impact on various domains, including:

- **Smart Homes:** Sensors monitor and control lighting, temperature, security systems, and appliances, making homes more energy-efficient and secure.
- **Industrial IoT (IIoT):** In manufacturing, sensors enable predictive maintenance, quality control, and automation, optimizing production processes.
- **Healthcare:** Wearable sensors and medical devices track vital signs, providing continuous monitoring and early disease detection.
- **Smart Cities:** IoT is used for traffic management, waste collection, energy conservation, and environmental monitoring, making cities more efficient and sustainable.
- **Agriculture:** Sensors help monitor soil conditions, crop health, and livestock, optimizing resource usage and increasing agricultural productivity.

Connecting the Internet of Things: A Dive into IoT Connectivity Technologies

The Internet of Things (IoT) has revolutionized the way we interact with technology and our surroundings, allowing everyday objects to communicate and exchange data seamlessly. At the core of this transformation are various IoT connectivity technologies, each with its unique characteristics and use cases. In this essay, we'll explore some of the key IoT connectivity technologies, including Wi-Fi, Bluetooth, Cellular, and LoRa, and understand how they enable the IoT ecosystem to thrive.

1. Wi-Fi (Wireless Fidelity):

Wi-Fi is one of the most familiar and widely used wireless communication technologies. It's known for its high data transfer rates and widespread availability in homes, offices, and public spaces. Wi-Fi-enabled IoT devices leverage existing infrastructure, making it a popular choice for smart homes and commercial applications. Key features of Wi-Fi in IoT include:

- **High Bandwidth:** Wi-Fi provides high-speed data transfer, suitable for applications like video streaming, online gaming, and real-time data transmission.
- **Local Area Coverage:** Wi-Fi typically covers a limited area, making it ideal for home networks, offices, and small businesses.
- **Power Consumption:** Wi-Fi consumes more power compared to some other IoT technologies, which may not be suitable for battery-powered devices.

2. Bluetooth:

Bluetooth is another well-known wireless technology, commonly used for short-range communications between devices. It's energy-efficient and suitable for IoT applications where low power consumption is essential. Key features of Bluetooth in IoT include:

- **Low Energy (BLE):** Bluetooth Low Energy (BLE) is a variant designed for power efficiency, making it suitable for IoT devices like wearables, beacons, and smart sensors.
- **Short Range:** Bluetooth has a relatively short operating range, typically up to 100 meters, making it suitable for local device connections.
- **Interoperability:** Bluetooth is supported by a wide range of devices, ensuring compatibility and ease of integration.

3. Cellular Networks:

Cellular networks, including 3G, 4G LTE, and the emerging 5G, provide ubiquitous connectivity over vast geographic areas. Cellular IoT is commonly used for applications that require broad coverage, mobility, and reliable data transfer. Key features of cellular networks in IoT include:

- **Global Coverage:** Cellular networks offer near-global coverage, making them suitable for tracking assets, vehicles, and remote monitoring in various industries.

- **High Data Rates:** 4G LTE and 5G provide high-speed data transfer, enabling real-time applications and video streaming.
- **Subscription Costs:** Cellular connectivity often involves subscription fees, which can be a consideration for cost sensitive IoT deployments.

4. LoRa (Long Range):

LoRa is a wireless communication technology designed for long-range, low-power IoT applications. It's particularly suitable for applications where devices are deployed in remote areas or where battery life is crucial. Key features of LoRa in IoT include:

- **Long Range:** LoRa can transmit data over several kilometers in rural areas, making it ideal for agriculture, environmental monitoring, and smart city applications.
- **Low Power:** LoRa devices can operate on battery power for extended periods, sometimes years, without frequent replacements.
- **Low Data Rates:** LoRa offers lower data rates compared to Wi-Fi or cellular, making it suitable for applications that don't require high-speed data transfer.

5. Other IoT Connectivity Technologies:

Apart from the mentioned technologies, IoT also employs other specialized connectivity options such as Zigbee, Z-Wave, Sigfox, and NB-IoT, each tailored to specific use cases and requirements.

IoT connectivity technologies are the lifelines of the IoT ecosystem, enabling devices to communicate, share data, and make our world more interconnected and intelligent. The choice of connectivity technology depends on various factors, including the application's range, power requirements, data transfer speed, and cost considerations. As IoT continues to evolve, new connectivity technologies and innovations will further expand the possibilities and impact of the IoT revolution. Whether it's Wi-Fi for your smart home, Bluetooth for your wearables, cellular for tracking assets, or LoRa for remote sensing, these technologies are collectively shaping the future of connected devices and the way we interact with our surroundings.

Connecting the Dots: IoT Protocols - The Language of the Internet of Things

The Internet of Things (IoT) has transformed the way we interact with and perceive the world around us. At the heart of this interconnected web of devices and systems are IoT protocols - the vital communication languages that enable devices to share data, coordinate actions, and empower the IoT ecosystem. In this essay, we'll explore some key IoT protocols, including MQTT, CoAP, HTTP, and others, understanding how they facilitate seamless communication within the IoT landscape.

1. MQTT (Message Queuing Telemetry Transport):

MQTT is a lightweight, efficient, and widely adopted publish-subscribe protocol designed for low-bandwidth, high-latency, or unreliable networks. It operates on a client-server model and is particularly well-suited for IoT applications. Key features of MQTT include:

- **Publish-Subscribe Model:** MQTT follows a publish-subscribe model, where devices (publishers) send messages to topics, and other devices (subscribers) receive messages from topics they are interested in.
- **Quality of Service (QoS):** MQTT offers different QoS levels to ensure message delivery reliability, making it suitable for both real-time and asynchronous communication.
- **Low Overhead:** MQTT's small message headers and minimal protocol overhead reduce the data transmission burden, making it ideal for low-power IoT devices.

2. CoAP (Constrained Application Protocol):

CoAP is designed for resource constrained IoT devices that require lightweight communication. It mirrors the principles of HTTP but is optimized for constrained environments. Key features of CoAP include:

- **Request-Response Model:** CoAP follows a request-response model similar to HTTP, making it easy to integrate with web services.
- **UDP-Based:** CoAP uses the User Datagram Protocol (UDP), reducing the overhead associated with TCP/IP and making it suitable for low-power devices.
- **Resource-Oriented:** CoAP identifies resources on devices using Uniform Resource Identifiers (URIs), simplifying resource management.

3. HTTP (Hypertext Transfer Protocol):

While HTTP is not exclusive to IoT, it plays a significant role in IoT communication, particularly in applications that require interoperability with web services. Key features of HTTP in IoT include:

- **Universal Compatibility:** HTTP is a well-established protocol, supported by virtually all devices and web services, making it ideal for IoT applications that require broad compatibility.
- **Stateless Communication:** HTTP operates in a stateless manner, which simplifies interactions between IoT devices and servers.
- **Secure Communication:** HTTPS (HTTP Secure) ensures secure data transmission between devices and web servers, crucial for sensitive IoT applications.

4. Other IoT Protocols:

Apart from MQTT, CoAP, and HTTP, there are several other IoT protocols, each designed for specific use cases and requirements:

- **AMQP (Advanced Message Queuing Protocol):** A message-oriented middleware protocol suitable for IoT applications requiring advanced queuing capabilities and message routing.
- **DDS (Data Distribution Service):** Designed for real-time, mission-critical IoT applications, DDS offers data-centric communication with high reliability and performance.
- **Websockets:** Provides full-duplex communication channels over a single TCP connection, ideal for real-time IoT applications that require bidirectional data flow.
- **Sigfox and LoRaWAN:** LPWAN (Low-Power Wide-Area Network) protocols designed for long-range, low-power IoT applications such as remote sensing and asset tracking.

IoT protocols serve as the invisible conduits that enable devices to communicate, share information, and collaborate within the vast IoT ecosystem. The choice of protocol depends on factors such as network constraints, device capabilities, data requirements, and application objectives. As IoT continues to evolve, the diversity of protocols will expand, offering developers a rich toolkit to build increasingly sophisticated and interconnected IoT solutions. These protocols are the languages of the IoT, enabling devices and systems to speak to each other, and in doing so, they are propelling the world into a new era of connected intelligence and innovation.

Cloud Computing and Edge Computing: Empowering the Internet of Things (IoT)

The Internet of Things (IoT) has ushered in a new era of connectivity, transforming the way we interact with devices, collect data, and make decisions in various domains, from industrial processes to smart homes and healthcare. Central to the success of IoT are two paradigms: cloud computing and edge computing. In this essay, we will explore the roles of cloud computing and edge computing in IoT, their advantages, and how they work together to create a powerful IoT ecosystem.

Cloud Computing in IoT:

Cloud computing has been a cornerstone of the IoT revolution, providing a scalable and cost-effective solution for managing and processing the enormous volumes of data generated by IoT devices. Here are some key aspects of cloud computing in IoT:

1. **Data Storage and Processing:** The cloud acts as a central hub where data from IoT devices is stored and processed. This offloads the resource-intensive tasks from the devices themselves, allowing them to focus on data collection and local processing.

2. **Scalability:** Cloud resources can be easily scaled up or down to accommodate varying workloads. This flexibility is crucial for IoT applications that experience fluctuating data volumes.
3. **Advanced Analytics:** Cloud platforms enable advanced data analytics, including machine learning and artificial intelligence, to derive valuable insights from IoT data. This supports predictive maintenance, anomaly detection, and optimization of IoT processes.
4. **Global Accessibility:** Cloud services are accessible from anywhere with an internet connection, allowing remote monitoring and control of IoT devices and applications.
5. **Data Security:** Cloud providers invest heavily in security measures, ensuring that data transmitted to and stored in the cloud remains protected. Encryption, access controls, and regular security updates are standard practices.

However, cloud computing also comes with certain limitations for IoT applications:

- **Latency:** Transmitting data to the cloud and receiving a response can introduce latency, which is undesirable in real-time or mission-critical IoT scenarios.
- **Bandwidth Constraints:** Large-scale IoT deployments can strain network bandwidth, causing delays and bottlenecks.
- **Privacy Concerns:** Storing sensitive data in the cloud raises privacy and compliance issues, particularly in healthcare and industrial settings.

Edge Computing in IoT:

Edge computing addresses many of the limitations associated with cloud computing in IoT by moving data processing closer to the source of data generation—near or at the edge of the network. Here's how edge computing benefits IoT:

1. **Low Latency:** Edge devices process data locally, reducing the time it takes to make decisions or respond to events. This is crucial for applications like autonomous vehicles and industrial automation, where split-second decisions are required.
2. **Bandwidth Optimization:** Edge computing reduces the need for transmitting vast amounts of raw data to the cloud. Instead, data is filtered and analyzed at the edge, conserving bandwidth.
3. **Real-Time Processing:** Edge devices can perform real-time analytics, enabling immediate actions and reducing dependence on cloud resources.
4. **Privacy and Security:** Edge computing allows organizations to keep sensitive data within their premises, enhancing data privacy and compliance with regulations.

However, edge computing also presents challenges:

- **Resource Constraints:** Edge devices may have limited computing power and storage, which can impact the complexity of data processing and analytics.

- **Management Complexity:** Distributing and managing edge devices in large-scale deployments can be more challenging than centralized cloud management.
- **Consistency and Scalability:** Ensuring consistent processing and scalability across diverse edge devices can be complex.

Cloud and Edge Computing Synergy in IoT:

In practice, cloud computing and edge computing are not mutually exclusive; they often complement each other. The synergy between these two paradigms enables organizations to harness the best of both worlds. For example:

- **Data Filtering:** Edge devices can filter and preprocess data, sending only relevant information to the cloud for further analysis.
- **Scalable Analytics:** Cloud resources can be used for complex, scalable analytics, while edge devices handle immediate, local processing.
- **Hybrid Architectures:** Organizations can adopt hybrid architectures that balance data processing between the cloud and edge based on specific application requirements.

Cloud computing and edge computing are integral to the success of IoT, providing the infrastructure and intelligence needed to make sense of the vast amount of data generated by IoT devices. While cloud computing offers scalability, advanced analytics, and global accessibility, edge computing addresses latency, bandwidth, and privacy concerns. The harmonious integration of these paradigms empowers organizations to create responsive, efficient, and secure IoT ecosystems that drive innovation and transform industries. As IoT continues to evolve, the dynamic interplay between cloud and edge computing will shape the future of connected devices and the way we interact with the world around us.

Chapter 3: Setting Up Your IoT Project : A Guide to Success

The Internet of Things (IoT) has revolutionized the way we interact with technology and the world around us. Whether you're an entrepreneur, a hobbyist, or a professional, embarking on an IoT project can be an exciting and rewarding endeavor. However, the journey to a successful IoT project begins with careful planning and execution. In this essay, we'll explore the key steps and considerations for setting up your IoT project.

1. Define Your Objectives:

The first and most critical step in setting up an IoT project is to define your objectives. Ask yourself:

- What problem or opportunity does your IoT project aim to address?
- What are your specific goals, both short-term and long-term?
- How will the project benefit end-users or stakeholders?

Clear objectives will guide every aspect of your project, from hardware selection to data analysis.

2. Select the Right Hardware:

Choosing the appropriate hardware components is crucial to your project's success. Consider:

- Sensors and actuators: Determine the types and quantity of sensors and actuators required for data collection and action implementation.
- Microcontrollers and processors: Select devices capable of running your application code and connecting to communication networks.
- Power sources: Ensure reliable and sustainable power supplies for your IoT devices, whether it's batteries, solar panels, or electrical outlets.
- Connectivity: Decide on the communication protocols and technologies (e.g., Wi-Fi, Bluetooth, LoRa, cellular) that best suit your project's needs.

3. Develop Software and Firmware:

Your IoT project will require software to control devices, collect data, and communicate with other systems. Key considerations include:

- Programming languages: Choose the most suitable programming languages for your microcontrollers and back-end systems.
- Data storage: Decide where and how you'll store the data generated by your IoT devices. Options include cloud platforms, local databases, or a combination of both.

- Security: Implement robust security measures to protect your devices and data from cyber threats.
- User interfaces: Develop user-friendly interfaces for device control and data visualization.

4. Connectivity and Communication:

Ensure that your IoT devices can communicate effectively. Consider:

- Network architecture: Design the network architecture that connects your devices to the internet and other devices.
- Data transmission: Implement reliable data transmission protocols to ensure data integrity.
- Data formats: Define standard data formats for consistent data interpretation and processing.

5. Data Management and Analysis:

Collecting data is only the first step. To derive insights and make informed decisions, focus on:

- Data analytics: Develop algorithms and analytics tools to process and interpret data.
- Visualization: Create dashboards or reports to present data in a meaningful way.
- Real-time processing: Consider real-time data processing for applications that require immediate actions or alerts.

6. Testing and Validation:

Thoroughly test your IoT devices and systems before deployment. Consider:

- Simulation: Simulate real-world conditions to identify and address potential issues.
- Scalability: Ensure that your solution can scale to accommodate a growing number of devices and data.
- User testing: Solicit feedback from end-users to improve user experience and functionality.

7. Deployment and Maintenance:

Deploy your IoT project to the target environment and maintain it over time. Key considerations include:

- Installation: Ensure proper installation and setup of your IoT devices.

- Monitoring: Implement remote monitoring and management tools to detect and resolve issues proactively.
- Updates and upgrades: Regularly update firmware and software to address vulnerabilities and add new features.

8. Data Privacy and Security:

Protecting the privacy and security of your IoT project is paramount. Consider:

- Data encryption: Encrypt data during transmission and storage to prevent unauthorized access.
- Access control: Implement access controls to restrict who can interact with your devices and data.
- Compliance: Comply with relevant data privacy and security regulations and standards.

9. Documentation and Knowledge Sharing:

Document your project comprehensively, including design choices, code, and maintenance procedures. Share knowledge with your team and the broader community to foster collaboration and innovation.

10. Continuous Improvement:

IoT projects are dynamic and ever-evolving. Continuously seek ways to improve your project, incorporating user feedback and emerging technologies to stay competitive and relevant.

In conclusion, setting up a successful IoT project requires a well-defined vision, careful planning, technical expertise, and ongoing commitment. By following these steps and staying adaptable to changing requirements, you can navigate the complexities of IoT development and bring your project to fruition, making a meaningful impact in the world of connected devices and data-driven innovation.

Selecting Hardware for IoT: Choosing the Right Platform for Your Project

The Internet of Things (IoT) has unleashed a wave of innovation, enabling a multitude of devices to connect and communicate with each other. One of the pivotal decisions in any IoT project is selecting the appropriate hardware platform. This choice significantly influences your project's capabilities, scalability, and overall success. In this essay, we will delve into the considerations and factors involved in selecting hardware for IoT, with a focus on popular platforms like Raspberry Pi and Arduino.

Understanding the IoT Hardware Landscape:

Before diving into specific platforms, it's essential to understand the IoT hardware landscape. IoT devices vary widely in terms of form, function, power requirements, and connectivity options. Here are some key factors to consider:

1. **Processing Power:** IoT devices range from low-power microcontrollers suitable for simple tasks to single-board computers capable of running full-fledged applications.
2. **Connectivity:** The choice of communication technologies (Wi-Fi, Bluetooth, LoRa, Zigbee, cellular, etc.) depends on the range, data requirements, and power constraints of your project.
3. **Power Source:** Some IoT devices are battery-powered, while others rely on mains electricity or energy harvesting techniques. Power efficiency is crucial.
4. **Cost:** Hardware costs can vary significantly, affecting the overall project budget.

Raspberry Pi:

The Raspberry Pi is a popular single-board computer known for its versatility, affordability, and robust community support. It's a suitable choice for IoT projects with the following characteristics:

- **Processing Power:** Raspberry Pi offers significantly more processing power than typical microcontrollers, making it suitable for applications that require data processing, analytics, or running complex software.
- **Connectivity:** Raspberry Pi models come equipped with Wi-Fi and Bluetooth, enabling easy network connectivity. Ethernet and cellular options are also available.
- **Customization:** You can expand Raspberry Pi's capabilities through various add-ons (HATs), sensors, and peripherals.
- **Operating System:** Raspberry Pi can run a variety of operating systems, including Raspberry Pi OS (formerly Raspbian), Linux distributions, and even Windows 10 IoT Core.
- **Community Support:** The Raspberry Pi community is vast and active, providing extensive documentation, tutorials, and forums for troubleshooting.

However, Raspberry Pi may not be the best choice for projects with stringent power requirements, as it is not as power-efficient as microcontrollers. Additionally, it may be overkill for simple, low-cost IoT deployments.

Arduino:

Arduino is a popular microcontroller platform known for its simplicity and ease of use. It is well-suited for IoT projects characterized by:

- **Low Power:** Arduino boards are designed to operate efficiently on low power, making them suitable for battery-powered IoT devices.
- **Real-time Control:** Arduino excels at real-time control applications, such as robotics and sensor interfacing.
- **Simplicity:** Arduino's programming environment is beginner-friendly and offers a quick learning curve for those new to electronics and coding.
- **Cost-Effectiveness:** Arduino boards are typically less expensive than Raspberry Pi models, making them an attractive choice for cost-sensitive projects.

However, Arduino's limited processing power and lack of built-in networking capabilities can be limiting for projects that require complex data processing and internet connectivity.

Factors for Consideration:

When selecting hardware for your IoT project, consider the following factors:

1. **Project Requirements:** Clearly define your project's objectives, data processing needs, and connectivity requirements.
2. **Power Constraints:** Assess whether your project needs to operate on battery power or can rely on a consistent power source.
3. **Cost:** Evaluate your budget and choose hardware that aligns with your financial constraints.
4. **Scalability:** Consider whether the chosen hardware can scale to accommodate a growing number of devices if needed.
5. **Community and Support:** Investigate the availability of resources, tutorials, and community support for your chosen platform.
6. **Prototyping:** If unsure, consider prototyping your IoT project with multiple platforms to determine the most suitable one.

Selecting the right hardware for your IoT project is a critical decision that impacts functionality, scalability, and project success. Whether you opt for Raspberry Pi, Arduino, or another platform, ensure that your choice aligns with your project's objectives, power constraints, budget, and scalability requirements. With careful consideration and a clear understanding of your project's needs, you can embark on your IoT journey with confidence and the right hardware in hand.

Installing Necessary Software for IoT Development: A Comprehensive Guide

The field of Internet of Things (IoT) development is thriving, with an ever-growing number of devices and applications connecting and transforming the world. However, harnessing the potential of IoT requires the installation of specific software and development platforms. In this essay, we will explore the essential software components and IoT development platforms needed to kickstart your IoT projects effectively.

Understanding IoT Development Software:

IoT development software encompasses a wide range of tools, libraries, and platforms tailored to build, deploy, and manage IoT applications. Here are the core software components you need:

1. **Integrated Development Environments (IDEs):** IDEs are essential for writing, debugging, and testing IoT application code. Some popular IDEs for IoT development include:
   - **Arduino IDE:** Ideal for programming Arduino boards.
   - **PlatformIO:** A cross-platform IDE compatible with various IoT platforms, including Arduino, ESP8266, and ESP32.
   - **Eclipse IoT:** An open-source IDE and toolset for developing IoT applications on various platforms.

2. **Microcontroller-Specific Software:** If you are working with microcontrollers, you'll need software specific to the hardware platform you've chosen. For example:
   - **Arduino Software (for Arduino boards):** Provides libraries and tools to program Arduino microcontrollers.
   - **Espressif IoT Development Framework (ESP-IDF):** Supports the development of applications for ESP8266 and ESP32 microcontrollers.
   - **Mbed OS:** An open-source operating system designed for ARM-based microcontrollers.

3. **IoT Protocols and Libraries:** IoT applications rely on communication protocols and libraries to exchange data efficiently. Common IoT protocols include MQTT, CoAP, and HTTP. Libraries like PubSubClient (for MQTT) and TinyDTLS (for CoAP) are essential for protocol implementation.

4. **Cloud Services:** Cloud platforms are vital for storing, processing, and analyzing IoT data. Major cloud providers like Amazon Web Services (AWS), Microsoft Azure, Google Cloud Platform (GCP), and IBM Watson IoT offer IoT-specific services and SDKs.

5. **Data Visualization and Analytics Tools:** IoT data is valuable when it can be visualized and analyzed. Tools like Grafana, Tableau, and Apache Spark are instrumental in extracting insights from IoT data.

Installing and Setting Up IoT Development Software:

The process of installing IoT development software may vary depending on your chosen platform and tools. However, the following steps provide a general guideline:

- **Select the Right Development Environment:**
  Choose an IDE or development environment that suits your project and hardware platform. Download and install it from the official website or repositories.

- **Install Microcontroller-Specific Software:**
  If you are working with microcontrollers like Arduino or ESP8266/ESP32, follow the installation instructions provided by the respective platforms. This often includes downloading and installing drivers, IDE extensions, and board support packages.

- **Set Up IoT Protocols and Libraries:**
  To implement IoT communication protocols and libraries, you can use package managers like Arduino Library Manager or Python's pip. These tools simplify the installation process and ensure dependencies are met.

- **Configure Cloud Services:**
  Sign up for a cloud service provider account and create an IoT project. Follow the provider's documentation to set up the necessary credentials and integration with your development environment.

- **Integrate Data Visualization and Analytics Tools:**
  Depending on your data visualization and analytics requirements, you may need to install software like Grafana, Tableau, or Apache Spark on your development machine or cloud servers. Follow their respective installation guides.

- **Version Control and Collaboration:**
  Consider using version control systems like Git to manage your IoT project's source code. Collaborative platforms like GitHub or GitLab facilitate team collaboration and code sharing.

Best Practices for Software Installation:

- **Keep Software Updated: Regularly** update your development tools and libraries to access the latest features, security patches, and bug fixes.

- **Use Virtual Environments:** If you are working with multiple IoT projects or different software versions, consider using virtual environments (e.g., Python's virtualenv) to isolate project dependencies.

- **Backup Your Work:** Regularly back up your IoT project code, configurations, and documentation to prevent data loss.

- **Follow Security Best Practices:** Ensure that your software and development environment adhere to security best practices to protect your IoT applications and data.

- **Leverage Online Resources:** Online forums, documentation, and community support can be invaluable when facing installation or configuration challenges. Don't hesitate to seek help from the IoT developer community.

Installing the necessary software for IoT development is a crucial step in realizing the potential of IoT applications. By carefully selecting and setting up the right development tools, libraries, and platforms, you can streamline your IoT project's development process, enhance collaboration, and maximize the value of IoT data. With the proper software foundation in place, you can embark on your IoT journey with confidence, knowing that you have the tools and resources needed to bring your innovative IoT ideas to life.

Building the Foundation: Basic Hardware Setup for Your IoT Project

The Internet of Things (IoT) has ushered in a new era of connectivity, enabling a wide range of devices to communicate and interact with the digital world. At the heart of every successful IoT project lies a well-structured and efficient hardware setup. In this essay, we will explore the fundamental elements of a basic hardware setup for your IoT project, including sensors, microcontrollers, power sources, and communication interfaces.

1. Microcontroller or Single-Board Computer (SBC):

The microcontroller or single-board computer (SBC) serves as the brain of your IoT device, controlling its operation and data processing. Popular choices for IoT projects include:

- **Arduino:** Ideal for beginners and simple IoT applications, Arduino boards are easy to program and offer a wide range of sensors and shields for expansion.
- **Raspberry Pi:** Raspberry Pi is a versatile SBC capable of running complex applications and handling multiple sensors and peripherals.
- **ESP8266 and ESP32:** These microcontrollers are popular for low-power IoT projects and offer built-in Wi-Fi connectivity.

Select a microcontroller or SBC that aligns with your project's processing power, memory, and connectivity requirements.

2. Sensors and Actuators:

Sensors are the eyes and ears of your IoT project, enabling it to collect data from the physical world. The choice of sensors depends on your project's objectives and the environmental parameters you need to monitor. Common IoT sensors include:

- **Temperature Sensors:** For measuring ambient or object temperatures.
- **Humidity Sensors:** To monitor humidity levels in the air.
- **Motion Sensors:** Used for detecting movement or changes in position.
- **Light Sensors:** For measuring light intensity or ambient light levels.
- **Proximity Sensors:** To detect the presence or absence of objects.
- **Gas Sensors:** Used for detecting the presence and concentration of gases.
- **Other Specialized Sensors:** Such as sound, vibration, pressure, or image sensors, depending on your project's needs.

Actuators, on the other hand, are responsible for taking actions based on data collected by sensors. Common IoT actuators include motors, servos, solenoids, and relays.

3. Power Source:

Selecting the appropriate power source is crucial for ensuring your IoT device operates reliably. Depending on your project's power requirements and constraints, consider the following options:

- **Battery Power:** Ideal for portable and low-power IoT devices. Choose rechargeable or non-rechargeable batteries based on your project's longevity needs.
- **Solar Power:** In remote or outdoor IoT deployments, solar panels can provide a sustainable source of energy, especially in combination with batteries or energy storage solutions.
- **Mains Power:** For devices installed in fixed locations with access to electrical outlets, mains power is a reliable option.

Efficient power management and conservation techniques are essential to prolong the operational life of battery powered IoT devices.

4. Communication Interfaces:

To transmit data from your IoT device to the cloud or other devices, you'll need appropriate communication interfaces. Common IoT communication options include:

- **Wi-Fi:** Enables high-speed, reliable internet connectivity for devices within Wi-Fi network range.
- **Bluetooth:** Suitable for short-range, low-power communication between devices.
- **Cellular:** Ideal for remote or mobile IoT deployments, offering wide coverage but typically higher power consumption.
- **LoRa (Low-Power Wide-Area Network):** Designed for long-range, low-power IoT applications, particularly in agriculture, environmental monitoring, and asset tracking.

Choose a communication interface that aligns with your project's data transfer requirements, range, and power efficiency.

5. Housing and Enclosures:

Protecting your IoT hardware from environmental factors such as dust, moisture, and temperature variations is essential. Consider using appropriate enclosures or housings to safeguard your IoT devices. The material and design of the enclosure should be selected based on the specific environmental conditions your IoT device will encounter.

6. Mounting and Placement:

Determine where and how your IoT device will be mounted or placed in its target environment. Proper mounting and placement are critical to ensuring sensors collect accurate data and actuators perform their tasks effectively.

7. Wiring and Connectivity:

Plan the wiring and connectivity of sensors, actuators, and power sources to the microcontroller or SBC. Organize and label connections to simplify troubleshooting and maintenance.

The hardware setup is the foundation upon which your IoT project is built. By carefully selecting the right microcontroller or SBC, sensors, power source, communication interfaces, enclosures, and mounting methods, you create a robust and reliable platform for your IoT device. Attention to detail in the hardware setup phase will set the stage for successful data collection, processing, and communication in your IoT project, enabling you to achieve your project's objectives and unlock the full potential of IoT technology.

Chapter 4: IoT Data Collection

Harnessing the Flow: IoT Data Collection in the Age of Connectivity

The Internet of Things (IoT) has become an integral part of our modern world, revolutionizing the way we interact with technology and gather information. At the core of this transformation lies IoT data collection, a process that empowers businesses, industries, and individuals with unprecedented insights into the physical world. In this essay, we'll delve into the significance, challenges, methods, and best practices of IoT data collection.

The Significance of IoT Data Collection:

IoT data collection serves as the bridge between the physical and digital realms, enabling the extraction of valuable information from sensors, devices, and objects in the real world. The significance of IoT data collection can be summarized in several key points:

1. **Informed Decision-Making:** By collecting data from diverse sources, IoT allows for data-driven decision-making, facilitating more accurate, timely, and context-aware actions.
2. **Operational Efficiency:** Businesses and industries can optimize processes, predict maintenance needs, and reduce downtime through real-time data collection, resulting in cost savings and improved productivity.
3. **Improved User Experiences:** IoT data collection enhances user experiences through personalized services, responsive environments, and adaptive systems.
4. **Sustainability:** IoT data helps monitor and manage resources more efficiently, contributing to sustainability efforts by reducing waste and energy consumption.

While IoT data collection offers significant benefits, it also presents various challenges:

1. **Data Volume:** IoT generates enormous amounts of data, requiring scalable storage and processing solutions.
2. **Data Variety:** IoT data comes in various formats and structures, from sensor readings to multimedia content, requiring flexible data management.
3. **Data Velocity:** Real-time data collection demands low-latency communication and processing capabilities to support time-sensitive applications.
4. **Data Security and Privacy:** Protecting sensitive IoT data from cyber threats and ensuring user privacy are paramount concerns.

IoT data collection methods encompass a range of technologies and techniques:

1. **Sensor Networks:** IoT relies on sensors to collect data from physical environments. These sensors can include temperature sensors, motion detectors, cameras, and more.

2. **Gateways and Edge Devices:** Data collected by sensors is transmitted to gateways or edge devices, which preprocess and filter data before sending it to the cloud or a central server.
3. **Connectivity Technologies:** Various connectivity technologies, including Wi-Fi, cellular networks, Bluetooth, Zigbee, and LoRaWAN, facilitate data transmission between devices and central systems.
4. **Cloud Services:** Cloud platforms store, process, and analyze IoT data, offering scalability and accessibility from anywhere with an internet connection.
5. **Fog and Edge Computing:** Fog and edge computing enable data processing to occur closer to the data source, reducing latency and enabling real-time decision-making.

To ensure effective IoT data collection, consider the following best practices:

1. **Data Quality:** Implement data validation and cleaning mechanisms to maintain data accuracy and reliability.
2. **Data Security:** Encrypt data during transmission and storage, enforce access controls, and regularly update security measures.
3. **Scalability:** Design your data collection infrastructure to scale easily as data volume and device numbers grow.
4. **Data Governance:** Establish clear data ownership, access policies, and data retention policies to maintain data integrity and compliance with regulations.
5. **Data Localization:** Determine whether data processing should occur at the edge or in the cloud based on latency requirements and data volume.
6. **User Consent:** Respect user privacy by obtaining explicit consent for data collection and provide transparency about data usage.

IoT data collection is the lifeblood of the IoT ecosystem, serving as the foundation for informed decision-making, operational efficiency, improved user experiences, and sustainability efforts. While challenges such as data volume, variety, velocity, and security persist, IoT continues to evolve with innovative technologies and practices. As the IoT landscape matures, the effective collection, management, and analysis of IoT data will be crucial for unlocking the full potential of this transformative technology, shaping a smarter, more connected, and data-driven future.

Sensors and Data Acquisition: Unveiling the Power of Connected Sensors

The Internet of Things (IoT) represents a paradigm shift in how we interact with the world, enabling everyday objects and devices to collect and share data in ways previously unimaginable. Central to this transformation are sensors and data acquisition systems, the frontline troops of IoT data collection. In this essay, we will delve into the pivotal role of sensors and data acquisition in IoT data collection, exploring their significance, types, challenges, and best practices.

The Significance of IoT Data Collection on Sensors:

Sensors are the sensory organs of IoT, converting real-world phenomena into digital data. IoT data collection on sensors is significant for several reasons:

1. **Data Context:** Sensors provide the context needed to understand the physical world, from temperature and humidity to motion and sound, enriching the value of collected data.
2. **Real-Time Insights:** Sensors enable the continuous and real-time monitoring of environments, processes, and assets, allowing for prompt responses and predictive analytics.
3. **Precision and Accuracy:** Modern sensors offer high precision and accuracy, contributing to the reliability and quality of data collected.
4. **Diversity of Applications:** Sensors are versatile, with applications spanning agriculture, healthcare, manufacturing, smart cities, and more, making IoT data collection invaluable across industries.

Types of Sensors for IoT Data Collection:

Sensors come in various types, each suited to specific data collection needs:

1. **Environmental Sensors:** These include temperature sensors, humidity sensors, air quality sensors, and atmospheric sensors used to monitor and control environmental conditions.
2. **Motion Sensors:** Passive infrared (PIR), accelerometers, gyroscopes, and ultrasonic sensors detect motion and changes in position, essential for security, robotics, and navigation.
3. **Biometric Sensors:** Fingerprint sensors, heart rate monitors, and facial recognition sensors gather biometric data for authentication and health applications.
4. **Image and Video Sensors:** Cameras, image sensors, and video cameras capture visual data for surveillance, computer vision, and image analysis.
5. **Sound and Acoustic Sensors:** Microphones and acoustic sensors collect sound data, utilized in applications like voice recognition and noise monitoring.
6. **Chemical Sensors:** Gas sensors, pH sensors, and chemical analyzers detect chemical properties, vital in environmental monitoring, industrial safety, and healthcare.
7. **Proximity and Position Sensors:** Proximity sensors, GPS modules, and position sensors determine the distance between objects and their precise location.

Challenges in IoT Data Collection on Sensors:

IoT data collection on sensors presents unique challenges:

1. **Data Volume:** Sensors can generate massive data volumes, necessitating efficient data storage and processing solutions.
2. **Data Variety:** Diverse sensor types produce data in various formats, requiring flexible data integration and management.
3. **Data Velocity**: Real-time data from sensors demands low-latency communication and processing for time-critical applications.
4. **Data Quality:** Ensuring data accuracy and reliability is essential, as sensor data errors can have serious consequences.

To harness the power of IoT data collection on sensors effectively, adhere to these best practices:

1. **Sensor Selection**: Choose sensors tailored to your specific use case, considering factors like accuracy, range, and power consumption.
2. **Data Calibration:** Regularly calibrate sensors to maintain data accuracy and consistency.
3. **Data Validation:** Implement validation mechanisms to identify and mitigate erroneous or outlier data points.
4. **Data Compression:** Employ data compression techniques to reduce the volume of data transmitted, especially in bandwidth-constrained scenarios.
5. **Data Security:** Secure sensor data with encryption during transmission and storage and enforce access controls.
6. **Data Aggregation:** Use edge computing or gateways for preliminary data aggregation and filtering before transmitting to the cloud.
7. **Data Visualization:** Visualize sensor data through dashboards and analytics tools for meaningful insights and decision-making.

Safeguarding the Data Highway: IoT Data Transmission and Security Considerations

In the age of the Internet of Things (IoT), where billions of devices communicate seamlessly, data transmission and security have become paramount. IoT data is the lifeblood of connected systems, and ensuring its secure and efficient flow is essential. This essay explores the intricacies of IoT data transmission and the critical security considerations that must accompany it.

The Significance of IoT Data Transmission:

IoT data transmission refers to the process of sending data from IoT devices to central servers, cloud platforms, or other connected devices. The significance of this transmission lies in several key aspects:

1. **Real-time Insights:** IoT data transmission enables the real-time collection and analysis of data, facilitating immediate decision-making and action.

2. **Remote Monitoring:** IoT devices can transmit data from remote or inaccessible locations, allowing for monitoring and control without physical presence.
3. **Data Aggregation:** Multiple IoT devices can transmit data to a centralized system, enabling the aggregation of data for comprehensive analysis and reporting.
4. **Scalability:** IoT data transmission systems must scale to accommodate the growing number of devices and data volume, making efficient data transfer vital.

IoT Data Transmission Methods:

IoT data transmission can take various forms, depending on factors like device type, communication range, and power efficiency:

1. **Wi-Fi:** Commonly used for local communication within a home or business network, Wi-Fi provides high data rates and is suitable for devices with consistent power sources.
2. **Bluetooth:** Ideal for short-range communication between devices, Bluetooth is energy-efficient and widely used in applications like wearables and smart home devices.
3. **Cellular Networks:** Cellular communication offers extensive coverage, making it suitable for remote or mobile IoT deployments. However, it may consume more power than other methods.
4. **LoRa (Low-Power Wide-Area Network):** LoRa is designed for long-range, low-power IoT applications, such as agriculture, environmental monitoring, and asset tracking.
5. **MQTT and CoAP:** Protocols like MQTT (Message Queuing Telemetry Transport) and CoAP (Constrained Application Protocol) enable efficient data transmission and are commonly used in IoT.

Security Considerations in IoT Data Transmission:

IoT data transmission presents unique security challenges that must be addressed:

1. **Data Encryption:** Encrypt data during transmission to protect it from interception or tampering. TLS (Transport Layer Security) and DTLS (Datagram Transport Layer Security) are common encryption protocols.
2. **Authentication:** Implement strong authentication mechanisms to ensure that only authorized devices can transmit and receive data.
3. **Access Control:** Enforce access control policies to restrict who can access and modify data during transmission.
4. **Device Identity:** Assign unique identities to IoT devices and employ device authentication to verify their legitimacy.
5. **Data Integrity:** Use checksums and hashing to verify data integrity, ensuring that data has not been altered during transmission.
6. **Secure Protocols:** Select secure communication protocols like MQTT over TLS or CoAP with DTLS to protect data in transit.

7. **Firewalls and Intrusion Detection:** Employ firewalls and intrusion detection systems to monitor and protect data transmission channels.
8. **Firmware Updates**: Ensure that IoT devices can receive secure firmware updates to patch vulnerabilities and improve security.

Best Practices for Secure IoT Data Transmission:

To enhance IoT data transmission security, consider these best practices:

1. **End-to-End Encryption:** Implement end-to-end encryption to protect data from the moment it is generated to its final destination.
2. **Regular Auditing:** Regularly audit and update security measures to address emerging threats and vulnerabilities.
3. **Data Minimization:** Transmit only necessary data to reduce the attack surface and conserve bandwidth.
4. **Secure Boot and Firmware Validation:** Ensure devices have secure boot processes and validate firmware integrity during updates.
5. **Security by Design**: Integrate security into the IoT system's design, rather than attempting to add it as an afterthought.

IoT data transmission is the backbone of connected systems, enabling real-time insights, remote monitoring, data aggregation, and scalability. However, ensuring the security of IoT data during transmission is paramount, given the diverse range of devices and communication methods involved. By implementing strong encryption, authentication, access control, and monitoring mechanisms, organizations can safeguard the data highway and protect IoT data from unauthorized access, interception, or tampering. As IoT continues to expand its influence, secure data transmission will remain a cornerstone of building trust and reliability in the interconnected world.

Chapter 5: IoT Communication Protocols

The Internet of Things (IoT) is a vast network of interconnected devices, enabling them to communicate and share data seamlessly. Communication protocols form the backbone of this network, defining the rules and standards that facilitate data exchange among IoT devices. These protocols ensure efficient, secure, and reliable communication, allowing diverse devices to interact and collaborate in various applications.

Importance of IoT Communication Protocols

Imagine a world where devices from different manufacturers, using various technologies, attempt to communicate without a common language. This scenario underscores the critical role of IoT communication protocols in enabling interoperability and seamless connectivity among devices.

Key Objectives of IoT Protocols:

1. **Interoperability:** IoT protocols enable devices from different vendors to communicate and collaborate regardless of their underlying technology or hardware.
2. **Efficiency:** Efficient protocols optimize data transmission, minimizing latency and conserving resources like power and bandwidth.
3. **Security:** Robust security mechanisms embedded within protocols ensure data integrity, confidentiality, and authentication to prevent unauthorized access and data breaches.
4. **Scalability:** Protocols must accommodate the exponential growth of IoT devices, allowing the network to expand without compromising performance.

Common IoT Communication Protocols

Several protocols cater to the diverse needs of IoT applications, each designed with specific characteristics suited for different scenarios:

1. **MQTT (Message Queuing Telemetry Transport):** Known for its lightweight nature, MQTT is ideal for constrained environments where bandwidth and power are limited. It follows a publish-subscribe model, facilitating efficient one-to-many communication.
2. **HTTP/HTTPS (Hypertext Transfer Protocol/Secure):** Widely used in web applications, these protocols are suitable for IoT applications that require data retrieval or control via web interfaces. HTTPS ensures data security through encryption.

3. **CoAP (Constrained Application Protocol):** Designed for resource-constrained devices, CoAP is a lightweight protocol built on top of UDP, enabling efficient communication in IoT deployments with limited resources.
4. **AMQP (Advanced Message Queuing Protocol):** Ideal for scenarios requiring reliable and secure message queuing, AMQP facilitates message-oriented middleware, ensuring reliable delivery and interoperability.
5. **Bluetooth and Bluetooth Low Energy (BLE):** Often used in IoT devices for short-range communication, Bluetooth and BLE enable connectivity in personal area networks (PANs), commonly found in wearable devices and smart home applications.
6. **Zigbee and Z-Wave:** Both are wireless protocols optimized for low-power, short-range communication in smart home automation, providing mesh networking capabilities for connecting multiple devices.
7. **LoRaWAN (Long Range Wide Area Network):** Suited for long-range communication in IoT deployments, LoRaWAN enables low-power, wide-area networks suitable for applications like smart cities and agriculture.

Choosing the Right Protocol

Selecting the appropriate communication protocol for an IoT deployment depends on various factors:

- **Device Constraints:** Consider the device's processing power, memory, and energy requirements.
- **Data Requirements:** Evaluate the volume, frequency, and type of data exchanged by devices.
- **Security Needs:** Assess the sensitivity of data and the required level of security measures.
- **Network Topology:** Determine whether the deployment involves a centralized or decentralized network structure.

Conclusion

IoT communication protocols play a pivotal role in enabling seamless connectivity and data exchange among the vast array of interconnected devices. The choice of protocol depends on specific application requirements, device capabilities, and network constraints. As IoT continues to evolve, protocols will adapt and innovate to meet the dynamic needs of connected ecosystems, fostering innovation and advancement in various industries.

Chapter 6: Data Storage and Analysis in the IoT Era

In the vast landscape of the Internet of Things (IoT), data is the lifeblood that fuels insights, decisions, and innovations. As billions of devices generate an unprecedented volume and variety of data, robust mechanisms for storage and analysis become imperative to derive meaningful insights and value from this information deluge.

Importance of Data Storage and Analysis in IoT

IoT generates a staggering amount of data from diverse sources such as sensors, devices, applications, and users. Effectively storing and analyzing this data offer numerous benefits:

1. **Insight Generation:** Analyzing IoT data uncovers valuable insights, enabling organizations to make data-driven decisions, optimize processes, and innovate products and services.
2. **Predictive Capabilities:** Advanced analytics on historical and real-time IoT data empower predictive maintenance, forecasting, and trend analysis, preventing failures and optimizing operations.
3. **Enhanced Efficiency**: Data-driven insights optimize resource utilization, streamline operations, and improve overall efficiency across various industries, from manufacturing to healthcare.

Data Storage in IoT

Efficiently managing IoT data involves addressing challenges related to volume, velocity, variety, veracity, and value (the 5Vs of Big Data). Various storage technologies cater to the diverse needs of IoT data:

1. **Edge Computing:** Processing and storing data at the network edge reduce latency, minimize bandwidth usage, and enhance real-time decision-making by keeping critical data closer to the source.
2. **Cloud Storage:** Scalable cloud platforms offer vast storage capacities and computing power, providing flexibility, accessibility, and cost-effectiveness for storing and processing IoT data.
3. **Databases:** Specialized databases, such as time-series databases (optimized for timestamped IoT data) and NoSQL databases (for unstructured IoT data), accommodate different data formats and retrieval requirements.
4. **Distributed File Systems:** Technologies like Hadoop Distributed File System (HDFS) or distributed storage solutions enable the storage and processing of large-scale IoT data across clusters of nodes.

IoT Data Analysis

Analyzing IoT data involves extracting actionable insights, trends, and patterns. Various techniques and tools facilitate this process:

1. **Descriptive Analytics:** Summarizes past IoT data to understand historical trends, visualize data, and provide context for decision-making.
2. **Predictive Analytics:** Utilizes machine learning algorithms to forecast future outcomes, detect anomalies, and enable predictive maintenance in IoT systems.
3. **Prescriptive Analytics:** Offers actionable recommendations based on analyzed IoT data, guiding optimal decision-making in real-time.
4. **Streaming Analytics:** Analyzes real-time data streams from IoT devices, enabling immediate responses to emerging events or conditions.

Challenges and Considerations

Despite the immense potential, several challenges surround IoT data storage and analysis:

- **Security and Privacy:** Safeguarding IoT data against breaches, ensuring data integrity, and addressing privacy concerns remain critical challenges.
- **Scalability and Compatibility:** As IoT ecosystems expand, ensuring scalable storage and analysis solutions that are compatible with diverse devices and data formats becomes crucial.
- **Data Governance and Standards:** Establishing standards for data formats, interoperability, and governance frameworks are necessary for effective data utilization.

Conclusion

Data storage and analysis lie at the heart of deriving value from the vast troves of data generated by IoT devices. Effectively managing, storing, and analyzing this data empowers businesses, industries, and society at large to harness the transformative potential of the IoT, driving innovation, efficiency, and insights into every facet of our lives. As technology continues to evolve, the approaches to IoT data storage and analysis will likewise evolve, unlocking new possibilities and shaping the future of connected systems and intelligent decision-making.

Chapter 7: IoT Examples with Raspberry Pi

Raspberry Pi, a credit-card-sized computer, has gained immense popularity as a versatile and cost-effective tool for creating IoT solutions. With its GPIO (General Purpose Input/Output) pins, connectivity options, and community support, Raspberry Pi serves as an excellent platform for implementing a wide range of IoT applications. Here are several examples showcasing how Raspberry Pi can be used in IoT projects:

1. Home Automation

Raspberry Pi can function as a central hub for controlling smart home devices. Using compatible sensors, relays, and modules, it can manage lighting, temperature, security cameras, and smart appliances. For instance, you can build a system to automate lights based on motion detection or control home temperature using IoT-enabled thermostats.

2. Weather Station

Create a weather station using Raspberry Pi connected to sensors for measuring temperature, humidity, pressure, and rainfall. Collect data from these sensors and display it in real-time or store it for analysis. With the addition of a web server, you can publish this weather data online for remote access.

3. Smart Agriculture

Raspberry Pi can play a vital role in agricultural IoT applications. By integrating sensors for soil moisture, temperature, and humidity, it can monitor crop conditions. Automate irrigation systems based on real-time data to ensure optimal soil moisture levels, improving crop yield while conserving water.

4. IoT Security Camera

Transform your Raspberry Pi into a security camera by attaching a camera module and using software like MotionEyeOS. With the capability to connect to Wi-Fi or Ethernet, these cameras can stream footage, detect motion, and send alerts, enhancing home or office security.

5. Remote Monitoring and Control

Utilize Raspberry Pi to remotely monitor and control machinery or systems. For instance, you can build a system that remotely monitors and controls aquarium conditions by adjusting lighting, temperature, and feeding schedules based on sensor readings.

6. Smart Retail and Inventory Management

Implement IoT solutions in retail by using Raspberry Pi to monitor inventory levels with RFID or barcode scanners. This setup can automatically track stock levels, generate alerts for low inventory, and update inventory databases in real-time.

7. Education and Learning Projects

Raspberry Pi serves as an excellent educational tool for learning about IoT concepts, coding, and electronics. Educational kits and projects are available, enabling students to build IoT devices, understand sensor functionalities, and develop coding skills.

Conclusion

Raspberry Pi's affordability, versatility, and community support make it an ideal platform for exploring and implementing IoT applications. By leveraging its GPIO pins, connectivity options, and extensive software support, enthusiasts, hobbyists, educators, and professionals can create innovative IoT solutions across various domains. The examples provided here represent just a fraction of the vast possibilities that Raspberry Pi offers in the realm of IoT, empowering individuals to explore, learn, and innovate in the world of connected devices and systems.

Chapter 8: Real-Life IoT Use Cases

The Internet of Things (IoT) has revolutionized numerous industries, offering innovative solutions to enhance efficiency, safety, convenience, and sustainability. Here are some compelling real-life IoT use cases that illustrate the transformative impact of IoT across different sectors:

1. Smart Cities

Use Case: Smart Parking Systems

IoT-enabled sensors installed in parking spaces can relay real-time data to a centralized system. This information assists drivers in locating available parking spots via mobile apps, reducing traffic congestion and emissions while enhancing urban mobility.

2. Healthcare

Use Case: Remote Patient Monitoring

IoT devices like wearable sensors and monitors enable continuous monitoring of vital signs and health metrics. Healthcare providers can remotely track patients' conditions, enabling early intervention and personalized care, particularly for chronic disease management.

3. Agriculture

Use Case: Precision Agriculture

IoT sensors embedded in fields gather data on soil moisture, temperature, and crop health. Farmers use this data to optimize irrigation schedules, apply fertilizers, and make informed decisions, thereby increasing crop yield while conserving resources.

4. Manufacturing

Use Case: Predictive Maintenance

Sensors in industrial machinery collect data on performance and operating conditions. Predictive analytics analyze this data to predict potential failures, allowing for preemptive maintenance, minimizing downtime, and optimizing production efficiency.

5. Retail

Use Case: Inventory Management

Retailers use IoT devices like RFID tags and sensors to monitor inventory levels in real-time. This enables automated inventory tracking, reducing stockouts, improving supply chain efficiency, and enhancing customer satisfaction.

6. Energy Management

Use Case: Smart Grids

IoT devices and smart meters in energy grids monitor consumption patterns, allowing for efficient distribution of electricity. This optimization reduces wastage, balances loads, and integrates renewable energy sources, fostering sustainability.

7. Transportation and Logistics

Use Case: Fleet Management

IoT-enabled GPS trackers and sensors in vehicles streamline logistics operations. Fleet managers can monitor vehicle location, performance, and fuel efficiency, optimizing routes, reducing fuel consumption, and enhancing overall logistics efficiency.

8. Environmental Monitoring

Use Case: Air Quality Monitoring

IoT sensors deployed across cities measure air quality parameters in real-time. This data aids in assessing pollution levels, enabling authorities to take proactive measures to improve air quality and public health.

Conclusion

The implementation of IoT across various sectors demonstrates its potential to revolutionize industries by enabling data-driven decision-making, automation, and enhanced efficiency. These real-life use cases showcase how IoT technologies bring about tangible benefits, improving processes, services, and quality of life. As IoT continues to evolve, its impact on industries will deepen, leading to further innovations and transformative changes that shape the way we live, work, and interact with the world around us.

Chapter 9: IoT Security

The rapid proliferation of Internet of Things (IoT) devices has introduced unprecedented convenience and connectivity. However, it has also brought forth significant security challenges. Securing IoT devices and the data they generate is crucial to safeguarding privacy, preventing unauthorized access, and maintaining the integrity of systems. This chapter explores the complexities of IoT security and strategies to mitigate associated risks.

Unique Challenges in IoT Security

1. **Diversity of Devices:** IoT encompasses a vast array of devices with varying levels of security measures, making it challenging to maintain a uniform security standard across the ecosystem.
2. **Resource Constraints:** Many IoT devices operate with limited processing power, memory, and energy, which hinders implementing robust security protocols.
3. **Lack of Standardization:** The absence of universal security standards across IoT devices results in varying vulnerabilities and complexities in securing heterogeneous systems.

Key IoT Security Threats

1. **Unauthorized Access:** Weak authentication mechanisms and default credentials make IoT devices vulnerable to unauthorized access, potentially leading to data breaches or device manipulation.
2. **Data Privacy Concerns:** The collection and transmission of sensitive data by IoT devices pose privacy risks if not properly encrypted or protected.
3. **DDoS Attacks:** Compromised IoT devices can be harnessed into botnets, launching Distributed Denial-of-Service attacks that disrupt services by overwhelming networks or servers.
4. **Physical Security Risks:** The physical nature of IoT devices makes them susceptible to tampering, leading to security breaches or unauthorized control.

Strategies for IoT Security

1. **Device Authentication and Access Control:** Implement strong authentication methods like two-factor authentication and regularly update default passwords to prevent unauthorized access.
2. **Data Encryption:** Encrypt data both at rest and in transit to ensure confidentiality and protect against interception or tampering.
3. **Firmware Updates and Patch Management:** Regularly update device firmware and software to address vulnerabilities and apply security patches promptly.

4. **Network Segmentation:** Segment IoT devices into isolated networks to limit the impact of potential breaches and contain security risks.
5. **Security by Design:** Incorporate security measures into the design phase of IoT devices, considering principles such as least privilege, secure defaults, and fail-safes.
6. **Continuous Monitoring and Incident Response:** Implement robust monitoring systems to detect anomalies or suspicious activities and have a well-defined incident response plan in place.

Industry and Regulatory Efforts

Governments and industry bodies have initiated efforts to address IoT security concerns:

- **Regulatory Standards:** Introducing regulations and standards, such as GDPR (General Data Protection Regulation), to enforce security and privacy requirements for IoT devices.
- **Certification Programs:** Launching certification programs to verify the security compliance of IoT devices and encourage adherence to best practices.

Conclusion

IoT security is a multifaceted challenge requiring a holistic approach that encompasses device-level security, data protection, network integrity, and regulatory compliance. As the IoT landscape continues to evolve, stakeholders must prioritize security measures to mitigate risks and build trust in these interconnected systems. Collaborative efforts among manufacturers, regulators, and consumers are crucial to fostering a secure IoT environment that ensures privacy, safety, and reliability in our increasingly connected world.

Chapter 10: Future Trends in IoT

The Internet of Things (IoT) has evolved significantly, transforming industries and daily life. As technology advances and innovation accelerates, several trends are poised to shape the future of IoT, introducing new possibilities and opportunities. This chapter explores the emerging trends and potential developments that will redefine the IoT landscape.

1. Edge Computing Integration

Future Trend: Greater Adoption of Edge Computing in IoT

Edge computing will witness increased integration with IoT systems. By processing data closer to the source (IoT devices), edge computing reduces latency, optimizes bandwidth, and enhances real-time decision-making, especially in critical applications like autonomous vehicles and healthcare.

2. AI and Machine Learning Convergence

Future Trend: AI-Driven IoT Solutions

The convergence of Artificial Intelligence (AI) and IoT will become more pronounced. AI and machine learning algorithms will analyze vast amounts of IoT data to derive actionable insights, enable predictive analytics, and automate decision-making processes, thereby enhancing efficiency and innovation across industries.

3. 5G Connectivity

Future Trend: Accelerated Deployment of 5G for IoT

The rollout of 5G networks will significantly impact IoT by providing faster speeds, lower latency, and increased device connectivity. This high-speed, low-latency connectivity will support massive IoT deployments, enabling new applications and services that demand real-time data transmission.

4. Enhanced Security Measures

Future Trend: Advancements in IoT Security

Addressing security concerns will remain a top priority. Innovations in IoT security will encompass enhanced encryption methods, secure hardware modules, and the adoption of blockchain technology to ensure data integrity, confidentiality, and authentication across IoT ecosystems.

5. Interoperability and Standards

Future Trend: Focus on Interoperability and Standardization

Efforts to establish common standards and interoperability protocols will intensify. Collaboration among industry stakeholders to create unified standards will facilitate seamless connectivity and integration among diverse IoT devices and platforms.

6. Sustainability and Green IoT

Future Trend: Eco-Friendly IoT Solutions

There will be a growing emphasis on developing sustainable IoT solutions. Energy-efficient devices, smart resource management systems, and IoT applications aimed at environmental conservation will gain traction, contributing to a greener and more sustainable future.

7. Ubiquitous IoT Integration

Future Trend: Integration of IoT into Everyday Life

IoT integration will become even more pervasive in daily life. Smart homes, connected vehicles, wearable devices, and IoT-enabled healthcare solutions will seamlessly integrate into people's lives, offering personalized experiences and convenience.

Conclusion

The future of IoT holds tremendous promise as it continues to evolve and innovate, shaping industries, economies, and societies. Edge computing, AI-driven analytics, 5G connectivity, robust security measures, interoperability standards, sustainability, and ubiquitous integration are key trends that will redefine IoT applications and experiences. The collaborative efforts of industry leaders, innovators, policymakers, and consumers will drive the evolution of IoT, unlocking new potentials and transforming the way we interact with technology in the coming years.

Chapter 11: IoT in Action

The practical implementation of Internet of Things (IoT) technologies across diverse sectors illustrates how these innovations are reshaping industries, improving efficiency, and enhancing experiences. This chapter delves into real-world examples showcasing IoT applications in action.

1. Smart Agriculture: Crop Monitoring

Application: IoT sensors monitor soil moisture, temperature, and crop health in agricultural fields. This data is transmitted to farmers' devices, enabling precise irrigation scheduling and targeted resource utilization, thereby increasing crop yield and conserving water.

2. Healthcare: Remote Patient Monitoring

Application: Wearable IoT devices equipped with sensors continuously monitor patients' vital signs and health metrics. Healthcare providers receive real-time data, enabling remote patient management, early detection of anomalies, and personalized care, particularly for chronic disease management.

3. Smart Cities: Intelligent Traffic Management

Application: IoT sensors embedded in road infrastructure monitor traffic flow, congestion, and vehicle density. This data is analyzed in real-time to optimize traffic signal timings, reroute vehicles, and improve overall traffic management, reducing congestion and travel time.

4. Manufacturing: Predictive Maintenance

Application: IoT sensors in industrial machinery collect data on performance and operating conditions. Advanced analytics predict potential failures, enabling predictive maintenance schedules that minimize downtime, optimize equipment efficiency, and reduce maintenance costs.

5. Retail: Smart Inventory Management

Application: RFID tags and IoT sensors track inventory levels in real-time. Automated inventory systems monitor stock, generate alerts for low inventory, and optimize supply chain operations, ensuring accurate inventory levels and reducing out-of-stock situations.

6. Energy Management: Smart Grids

Application: IoT devices and smart meters in energy grids monitor consumption patterns. This data facilitates efficient electricity distribution, load balancing, integration of renewable energy sources, and optimizing energy usage, contributing to a more sustainable energy ecosystem.

7. Environmental Monitoring: Air Quality Sensing

Application: IoT sensors placed across urban areas measure air quality parameters in real-time. This data aids in assessing pollution levels, enabling authorities to take proactive measures to improve air quality and public health.

8. Transportation: Fleet Management

Application: GPS-enabled IoT trackers in vehicles monitor location, performance, and fuel efficiency. Fleet managers optimize routes, monitor driver behavior, and schedule maintenance, enhancing logistics efficiency and reducing operational costs.

Conclusion

The practical deployment of IoT solutions across various sectors demonstrates their tangible impact on efficiency, productivity, sustainability, and quality of life. These real-world applications showcase the transformative power of IoT technologies, optimizing processes, improving decision-making, and enabling innovations that reshape industries and societal experiences. As IoT continues to evolve, its applications will expand, bringing forth further advancements and unlocking new potentials for a more connected, efficient, and intelligent world.

Chapter 12: Getting Started with Your IoT Project

Embarking on an Internet of Things (IoT) project can be an exciting endeavor, whether you're a hobbyist, a student, or a professional looking to innovate. This chapter provides a step-by-step guide to help you get started with your IoT project.

1. Define Your Project Idea and Objectives

- **Identify Your Goal:** Determine the problem you want to solve or the application you want to create using IoT.
- **Clarify Objectives:** Define the specific outcomes or functionalities your IoT project should achieve.

2. Select Your IoT Platform or Device

- **Research IoT Platforms:** Explore different IoT platforms or devices (e.g., Raspberry Pi, Arduino, ESP8266) based on your project requirements.
- **Consider Features:** Choose a platform that aligns with your project's connectivity, sensor compatibility, and computing needs.

3. Plan Your Hardware Setup

- **List Required Components:** Make a list of sensors, actuators, controllers, and other hardware needed for your project.
- **Create a Schematic:** Sketch a schematic or diagram outlining the connections and interactions between components.

4. Set Up Your Development Environment

- **Install Necessary Software:** Download and install the required software development tools, IDEs (Integrated Development Environments), and libraries for your selected IoT platform.

5. Learn Programming and Prototyping

- **Understand Programming Languages:** Familiarize yourself with programming languages commonly used in IoT projects (e.g., Python, C/C++, JavaScript).
- **Practice Prototyping:** Start with simple projects to understand how to interface with sensors, read data, and control outputs using your chosen platform.

6. Connect to IoT Services or Cloud Platforms

- **Choose IoT Services:** Explore cloud - based IoT platforms (e.g., AWS IoT, Google Cloud IoT, Azure IoT) for data storage, analytics, and remote device management.
- **Set Up Connectivity:** Configure your device to connect to the chosen IoT platform or services.

7. Develop Your IoT Project

- **Write Code and Implement Features:** Develop the software for your IoT project, integrating sensor data, processing logic, and desired functionalities.
- **Test Iteratively:** Test each component and functionality of your project iteratively to identify and resolve issues.

8. Ensure Security Measures

- **Implement Security Protocols:** Incorporate security practices such as encryption, secure authentication, and regular updates to protect your IoT project from potential vulnerabilities.

9. Deploy and Monitor

- **Deploy Your Project:** Deploy your IoT project in the desired environment or location where it will be operational.
- **Monitor and Maintain:** Continuously monitor your project for performance, data accuracy, and potential issues. Regular maintenance and updates are essential.

10. Document and Iterate

- **Document Your Project:** Keep detailed records, including diagrams, code, and configurations, for future reference or improvements.
- **Iterate and Improve:** Collect feedback, analyze results, and iterate on your project to enhance functionality, efficiency, or user experience.

Conclusion

Starting an IoT project involves careful planning, learning, and hands-on experimentation. By following these steps and continuously learning and adapting, you can create innovative IoT solutions, whether for personal exploration, academic purposes, or professional development. The journey of building IoT projects is not just about the final product but also about the skills, experience, and insights gained along the way.

Chapter 13: Conclusion

The Internet of Things (IoT) has emerged as a transformative force, connecting the physical and digital worlds, revolutionizing industries, and reshaping our daily lives. This chapter encapsulates the essence of IoT, its impact, and the endless possibilities it presents.

IoT's Evolution and Impact

From its inception, IoT has evolved into a sprawling network of interconnected devices, sensors, and systems. It has transcended boundaries, permeating various sectors including healthcare, agriculture, manufacturing, smart cities, and more. The impact of IoT is profound:

- **Efficiency and Productivity:** IoT optimizes processes, enhances efficiency, and unlocks new levels of productivity by enabling data-driven decision-making and automation.
- **Innovation and Transformation:** IoT fuels innovation, giving rise to novel solutions and transforming industries, business models, and consumer experiences.
- **Improved Quality of Life:** IoT technologies improve quality of life through advancements in healthcare, smart homes, transportation, and environmental sustainability.

Challenges and Opportunities Ahead

While IoT offers immense promise, it also presents challenges:

- **Security Concerns:** Protecting IoT systems against cyber threats and ensuring data privacy remains a pressing challenge.
- **Interoperability and Standards:** Establishing common standards for interoperability among diverse IoT devices is essential for seamless integration.
- **Scalability and Sustainability:** As IoT deployments expand, ensuring scalability, energy efficiency, and environmental sustainability becomes crucial.

Future Prospects and Continuous Innovation

The future of IoT is brimming with possibilities:

- **Technological Advancements:** Edge computing, AI integration, 5G connectivity, and enhanced security measures will continue to drive IoT innovation.

- **Ubiquitous Integration:** IoT will become more integrated into everyday life, creating smarter homes, cities, transportation, and healthcare systems.
- **Human-Centric Approach:** IoT solutions will focus more on human needs, delivering personalized experiences and improving overall well-being.

Embracing the IoT Journey

As we navigate the evolving landscape of IoT, it's crucial to embrace its potential while addressing its challenges. Collaboration among industry leaders, innovators, policymakers, and consumers is vital to drive responsible and sustainable IoT development.

Whether you're a developer, entrepreneur, researcher, or consumer, understanding and harnessing the power of IoT opens doors to endless opportunities. The journey of IoT is marked not just by technological advancements but also by its societal impact and the way it transforms the world around us.

In conclusion, the continued evolution of IoT holds the promise of an interconnected world that is smarter, more efficient, and more responsive to our needs. By embracing innovation, fostering collaboration, and addressing challenges, we pave the way for a future where IoT enhances our lives and propels us toward greater achievements.

www.ingramcontent.com/pod-product-compliance
Lightning Source LLC
Chambersburg PA
CBHW080244260726
48658CB00008B/3224